The Feel Trio

LETTER ◆ MACHINE EDITIONS   TUCSON, AZ   DENVER, CO

The Feel Trio

FRED MOTEN

Acknowledgments:

Earlier versions of excerpts from "Block Chapel" were published in
Callaloo, *Hambone* and *A Public Space*; Earlier versions of excerpts from
"Come On, Get It!" were published in *Amerarcana* and *The Recluse*; and
an earlier version of "I ran from it and was still in it." was published
as a chapbook, with collages by Theodore A. Harris, by Cusp Books.

The poem in "Block Chapel" that begins "it would be this way" is
a variation on a theme by Amiri Baraka. That theme is given in his
poem "The New Invasion of Africa."

The poem in "Block Chapel" that begins "without saying another
word" is a distorted echo of some passages in Dianne Swann-Wright's
A Way Out of No Way: Claiming Family and Freedom in the New South.

In the first place, and when all is said and done, The Feel Trio is Cecil
Taylor, piano, William Parker, bass, and Tony Oxley, drums.

Published by Letter Machine Editions
Tucson, Arizona 85721
© 2014 by Fred Moten
All Rights Reserved
Book Design by HR Hegnauer
Cover art: "A Shirt" by Lorenzo Moten, Play-doh, 2009.
Printed in Canada
Cataloging-in-Publication Data is on file at the Library of Congress

ISBN: 978-0-9887137-1-0

lettermachine.org

Distributed to the trade by Small Press Distribution (spdbooks.org)

This book is for William Corbett.

block chapel

whenever I listen to cornelius I think of cecily
then fry then house then read the blacks with
peter pál. but sometimes it gets deep in the hold
and the cell's hard pleasure curls up in the water.
so I sail the dark river in the mind by rocket ship
(my high water everywhere is outer space, alabama)
and stay alive in the concept with an outbound feeling
of refuge, I'ma run, I'mo run, I'm gon' run to the city
of refuse, in russell's anarchy, for angola, by soas.
then bright dennis morris take my baby picture
and I'm risen in the balmed-out underground.
I get preoccupied with the tonal situation. I got
to kiss somebody to end up in the original. it's like
that outside drama is our knowledge of the world
and nobody claims it but us. we get it twisted
in the diagram. we know the score. we got a plan.

welcome to what we took from is the state.
welcome to kill you, bird. the welcome state
and its hurt world, where you been lost and tied,
bird. it's some hot water on the second floor
and the altar on the bottom is an ordered pair
of lemon chocolate on the curb. get jumped in.
enjoy the recital and the hospitality. come upon
surround recall the project rubble everywhere.
come up on some common operations. drink the
open of the open evening mix. english breakfast
and some curd and light whipping. get up on the
cooling board of new opposite steps and come
upon remains arranged by hand like an english
garden. cant to refuse the unsung isolation.
that sad impersonal personal shit that play off
every other frank but my little irregular frank,
his body shaped like an accordion, his body shaped
like a pear, in the every day feast day, but come up
on. you the one with so much work to do, merchant.
sing a shattered self is just a shelf, young captain,
sea? you perfectly welcome to what we give away.

played hymns for cinema and moth
and hot house epinonikon in a rocky
church with a club-bound feeling of
elbow. between the crack and pin
was my best friend except for the key
to the alternate noise. the key in the
folded message so the ground can talk.
the world waits every day for freedom
fighters and they come every day with
music in the delicate lofts with cats like
delicat and mantee and fragam playing
organ, flatted graven, rided for the rocket
in a chapel, the cats who can tell a story.

I made a book from the sky songs of bukka white.
it can't be read, but you can smile, but it ain't mine.
if you walk all over me I'mon' say how do you do.
the history of art from below is a violent greeting
on the surface of kansas city, a readymade social dance
upstairs in the gallery, baby, and tell 'em a rushing did it!
to burn for creative orchestra in köln, a block from
the konfrontationen in a ditch, with all this molecular
gastronomy and ceramics. the choir is a confection
circle. the kiln is an open form of worship on vine for
darkness. for the effervescent school of the desert is
sonny jones's brilliant needle, scratched on a wall
of cool leaning in his cryptograph for submarine
brush and hermitage, where they cut another line
for skywriting on a mirror on the ground, not to see
past you but to say good morning, not to belong to
my own parks but to not belong. vine is an expression
oven. pangiotto feels for me to the side and vine is
lifted. I'm a musician with metaphysical abilities.

her gold tooth with the elemental slide reveals that soul power is an ornament
of new bird come out in the open flood. can yopu appreciate that? or hear
the speech secrecy of the atlantic underbridge? it's still wandering; the potential
                              anarchy is still on tour, surrepetitious vamp just keep on coming to the rescue.
say you wanna blow? just let me blow. blow my thayang baby blow my thang wa
ditty say you wanna say say you wanna say say you wanna say say watch me say
I vocoded baby, I blew holes in fading, I grew cultures in a subterfuge. the effect
was enfolding twelve streams of base six digits like ba dc fe h that start to curl
in front, corner, harbor, verge, and counter. come go with me to my one time
                pad and get in the break of my project x as if I were a lys, like I'm a music lab,
am I an island dream? this is her extreme anthology, sometimes as design of what
they most examine, for wave, rushes, as pirates of enjoyment, who contemplate
and run in baltimore, in hambone telephone, remember?

without saying another word, a man who everyone by this time suspected had had a taste too much, with no cure for the spasms that shook her body and unsettled her life, when folks lived for christmas time, where they held onto it as a place of refuge (even if only in garrets and legal loopholes), with $7.12 as a time-based stream, waiting for twenty-three years in stephen trent's installation, because no one here is familiar with broodthaers and the refinements of spectatorship in brussels or lausanne or winesaps and oatmeal and a twenty-five cent hen the wezel killed, angered by the sight of a relative's table set with fancy white folks dishes, their translucence, yes this looks just like a white folks table to me, dumped the contents of a bowl onto the fancy tablecloth and ate the food directly from the cover. you can't do nothing with uncle lewis.

made rapid, in a city of frontage, off access, like an urgent cliff,
an outside chance of growing and forking, this whole problematic
of pottery and computing, I called you in my head, I should have
made a date, murray jackson in the water. life and death by water.
a strip of pitch to sound like endlessly slowing down in the freezing
water. the drummer has instructions for exhaustion in the sound
of making choices in the water. choice is in the water. detroit
is in the water. all y'all in the falling alter, your movie in the air

color brings the house down to carnival. another minute never ends.
falling is a choir brushing dirt up in our mouths. that transparence
till it's back down on the floor, raised up everything that was ever
taken anywhere, as emphatic grit with specific ribbons, curved in
grave red air and tilted back and forth between weave and hushed.

your coat is plain in light and the bottom is prepared to challenge
standing with texture and seeing but suddenly. that pattern on the
edge is graphic patience higgins on the edge so write him down like
smoke on paper and basic flavor. black smoke composition huddles
around the off chance, the sooty groove and the violent arco catalog.

let it go till it comes back again. it should be something on the wall. something on the floor should call itself when they break it down to put it back up again. when it comes back again it should be gone till it's all gone again and ready to return. it should pose and turn at the easy intersection till it can't come back again. repeat till it's all gone.

find the itinerant pasture in the wind. watch it sway against the neat cutting of irish lamb. its common grift is gone to the city, the steel mill and the nursing home, linked by diving to dumas and cow pastor, and made to suffer under imprecise grazing, cold executive gouging, brutal vacations and tight scheduled pretty songs like a crofter's ghost.

we study partial folds in them alpine jukes, bent, bow-tongued stick
and move and mahagonnic rupture in september, in alabama, throat
sung to the kabaret's general steppe and fade. out here you breathe
they breath, this bridge is just, this bridge is just a pile of bones this
load be breathing, this alpine rasp in this dry bridge just be weaving.

that's how fluxhall west got started, in head start. guerillas measured rhythm cloth for horus, dwight trible sang without a song. you'll see mothers from grape street and soul brothers from the strainelated fields of stanislaus, gilroy and dolores. valencia will be juicy and cool and hot and hunky. watch the choir step to that open macrophone.

just up from tupelo.
just ice jus grew little
sister. I'm little sister
from tallulah, just flew
in from don't you do

just about to pay
        just about to be okay
just about to run run runaway
    just about to go outside and play,

ruseiana, when you
move, you ruse, like
your big sister done,
just more precise,
just down from truro.

place is our new destitute imperative. place her trill inside. see if you can find a place.

you are the
flex principle
to build a new
impulse
in everyone

we propel we
drive the bloc
away it falls
away
we're carried away.

drive away the bloc experiment
it falls away we're
driven by what
we carry
drive away. fall out, engine, fallaway.

put fertile culture and unguarded
sediment from an island dairy
in a mixer with some stock
arrangements from the extra pieces.
call it the fugitive slave act.

in the cell
under singing
play a bunch of
different keep
on the sunny sides

place is our new
destitute imperative.
place her trill
inside. see if you
can find some place.

sit at my dinner table
tell me that your son
who teaches for america
says I remind him of
irving rhames

your hands are rough
from all that string
          and flour. improvise
the principle like
you have no interest

be together but not at the same time.
forget the contemporary scene and your
broken image. the corner is not the same
as being cornered. it's the other way.
be the other way to bring it around.

gridley the grindletonian,
I know you mad. keep
slinging that pink to red,
black scarf flowing, burnt
like a carl dix vibraharp

reach
for
the
cool silver
buckle

lace is our new
destitute imperative.
lace her trill
inside. see if you
can find some lace.

take your chance to make it up.
the sparkly blue is your engine.
the tree becomes your parapet.
the party that can make you fly.
you be the margin on the way.

fly
through
the
black
election

for a brush quartet and
atlas for open schooling
place it on our new
replace inside you
touch to open

place is our new destitute imperative. place her trill inside. see if you can find a place.

sound like a cat playing
extra inside the project.

make a close tear a tour,
but turn on that with
lewis turing,

monastic trail but tore off to the side, moravian bone from tarboro and salem, move
by lick retraction, in a refuge network, rehearsed on edgeware, like a machine that loves me but won't come see about me.
the music of electric wash, to make it music by saying so, so when you
write your name on me, in vespers, joëlle enjoying, with that ircamic attention to the sharp tenderness
between my fingers, my artificial intelligence, my chronic fuite, as steven
felt, aacmic transfer, accranic trane,

we can seize the time with functions, motherfucker, and I can wonder who I am, wake up beautiful, and know everything.

this landing was for smugglers. then we became smugglers. we put phonographs on the pylon and pearls in our hand for women's day. do you ever think about what it feels like to bury your own city again and again every evening in the evening air and have that shear taken for nothing by the ones who visit everyone but you?

the violence of the coping strata is specific and seasoned. we give
shit away to hurt people and build poor shelters that move and
wrap around. we love to hold the continual failure in one another,
till new things come from that like bullets that catch bullets for
butter and chocolate. our thing event theme is doin it to death.
I feel good is brazen on the scene of personal injury. sugar and spice
is some country-ass shit in the middle of this shit. I know I'm not
supposed to say it like that, but what about the rock fights and
random blades when language lays out? there's no language for the
too sweet object of everybody's third thought any muhfuckin way.
along those lines, do I remind you of your mother? I want to but
just to scare you. let's warm our hands in one another and feel the
long black arc of that absolute swing, fun and vulgar in the swung
self-stimulation of all them wrong, extra, diacritical names. I just
want to satisfy you; though you're not mine, you're not just mine.

communism is how you get nasty with enjoyment. good morning
is the new catastrophe of our boulevard. so you gave up what you
never had and now you're a collection agency. you need a lawyer.
at a loss, I say, good morning. he says, good morning. how are you?
good. how are you? good. we feel obscenely good about ourselves.

this brutal pleasure is what we have to give. what you waiting for
is in your hand if you hold it out. your absent haunting is nothing
special; the shit that's special is the residue. the cream. the burly
innovation. when you see it's worse than you could ever imagine
there's a dandelion. that's what hurts so goddamn much, the sun.

bitch rent is dysfunctional abdul talking loud.
long neurotic styles quarks pre-career
is color confinement, driving around in tanks,
a big-ass head in charge of included muddle.
but you a jaguar and remain the whole
of it. I miss your parties. they were hard for me
to be afloat there and remade for talking loud
'cause all that profile sound the same, gloss,
but curled up with a little tremolo when I walk.
the hard rock quiver of theory is on it and the
set-up, joe, is poetic waxing, hushed in the ear
of the informal organ, up against the organizer's
tough-ass love. the unexplainable is everything
and you can't turn to it 'cause it's always leaving.
it lives on as a shock to the system even though
it lives on as a shock to the system even though
the main thing is cool in the stream, hid below
a hand-drawn sign for the other fella, as if you
could compute some thing and fill up on the air
between, step by step, with joy and el, who is the
sound. living double is like seeing double, edge
indebted, octeted, lindon barretted, little drummered
little drummer, little ghetto in the combed-out
process of the new organic sun, the repossession
of south parkway in the open, here she come
stepping fast, fast, fast, black on black in black's
black-ass consent. her tongue is the main frame,
it's the next thing, the abstract first name. her village
is the main thing, her cathedral where the regal
is, off in the exframe, by where the real is, mr. anderson.

fugue segue hallway attic outcast dance
this pose this antique place with other
lines this crunk all good and skylit fold,
but I'm so sleepy I'm crazy, anne frank.
like freddie redd in the connection but
still waiting for the everyday start it up
of the works and instruments of waiting
till early evening and secret turning in
vague series till he turn until the turn
and then the door turn then we line
a stand with jams and arms like this and
take position in the count-off and fall
to work on the new machine from cross
the world and set out in delay's old apse.

the break experiment with beginning, shift for apprehension, till it show up gone, but we didn't believe in it anyway. just to get deep, to get invited to dance and study, like telescopes and computers do. they try to imagine what comes right after the big band. look how they curl up greeting and counting, lit up on the metanorth, astray in the propulsion lab, up under mt vernon alabama in bessemer's aftermath in magic in dominance in greeting and counting like dinah in scandinavia. all that little echoed pillow with others and nested, sweets on paper, where do it come from? how could it happen? it must have been there, giving and taking the form that can't be there, and now you open inside, and it's already broke so you can get inside, song by song.

this a service on the surface for frank wilderness and carl flippant.
my absolute beauty studies feelings in an open afterlife. I hold him
and I've lost and I feel it in my hands and the sharp distance of his
little bother, explosive flower of I'm not ready and I don't want to.
one of these things is not like the other one of them can ever understand
but I bet he won't try to understand it, which is sad, but that's who
church is for, to give yourself away to the mobile ocean, the hidden life of
the undecidable nightclub, in service and surface like jason's holiday.

fell off after while, laid out after a little while,
went up in the smokestack to watch it whirl.
this time was a different burn. made me wish
everybody's circle was in the air. if I had my
calluses I would play that, too. hard new lines
with broken lapses and sections for digging
and held to the rest of the edge for later on.
still thinking 'bout when we tore up the idea
with far and them in shadow bell and that
glass fade in the nest above the other studio.
the engineer came to see if I could hear them
play it back. I saw the circles and my circle fell
around them like a star inside a breath but open
at my fingers, which were soft, so I played myrrh.

it would be this way. so it wd be this way. you want it to be one way. that they wd get
a negro. look, a negro. we got a negro. there's a drone that looks like what we
want, a pretty wife, a prayer book for my passport, blew up

canting, severe from lounging, luxurious
meetings in bloody mosses and sandy ridge, in fort deposit   leaving where we stay and all we got. we can have some jobs,
for the other way and how we sound. but it's the other way   can we come to dinner? we want some money. we settled for
is how we sound. our musical breakfast is free. the bottoms   a negro. we settled in a house right by the fort. we're settlers.
walk and talk like ronnie boykins. our technique is feline   call us nathan. call me ethan. yassuh we can
and austere. no revenant box just roebuck, nail and wire, or black hammer,
hear the new composers crying? we make our thing more social than they thought.

the way orchestra sound in birmingham
that's my sound. I belong to that sound
all the time, everyday. how bound am I
by music! the brain's little wilderness is
a backbeat, a shotgun shack, a deferred
villa and built-in cross and time windows
and overlaid buzzes like you were struck
by the consolation of a blue joseph boye
when this seminar is on the discrepancy.
there's a theory of sound in the autograph
but you have to wait for the sound of the
                              theory of sound and fold it between
hands and presence in the upper room like   folded
a folded dream. the tower is held together
by every other building in town and the
mystery is in effect or an eremitic bridge
or a bridge machine or you'll know why.

come on and feel the liturgical east end of the city. an alarm takes you there through the hidden dollhouse arch to the half-circle flavor of roma, that romanesque smell, thumping in the house of the music on the run like a wrecking ball. they try to take it and they take it for pain and money. they show it and try to close it up inside and ship it all over the world. it's always something they can't get to but then they get to it and try to sell it so they can get to what was left. you just have to close your eyes and walk but they see everything and walk all over it like a bridge, on the shallow water, where we dance and eat and rub. everybody reaches out for you in the house party of abandoned buildings. they all steal because they've all been stolen. if you know that before you go in you can see yourself in every little step away, for the feast of ascension and rupture, thick layers of breath, twist and shout, to keep on making airshafts all night long. I just found out you can make the plans reflect this after the fact. if you wake up sad and faded, run look inside that tube. cobalt opens up like a crypt on the surface between knowing everything and all the new things you make up that nothing can ever know except the other ones who dance and eat and rub. but I just want to sit here with you if that's all right. you still got corn meal on your hands. there's a beautiful scale on your hands and a light walking away in the grove. there's a bump on the end of the joint if you can't make it home. sometimes but not all the time if you can't make it home. we carved it out almost by praying and it swelled from the edge of all that nail and string. I'm gon' sleep in there tonight myself, the city of god is too much more than whole, come on and dance and eat and rub.

come on, get it!

1

Performers feel each other differently,
as material things that never happen,

in persistent substance and their risen cities,

even if there's no escape. their training in certain clinical tendencies,

or in the general structure of being a problem,

because of the pivot they never disavowed
in throwness, begins the world where we are fallen,

falling down together in an accident we dream

a little section between one, not one and two, the impurity
        that found themselves, original derivative and fresh outside

                  at home, before the fact a little section

        eight, the upstairs row efficiency with a swimming pool, a little section
        sight

and look who's coming, it's the world's corrosion

2

                    the residual mirror and the drag
behind it,
the hesitate buzz in the interval,
          on the bias,
    at the zoning variance, juked manic,
                    gone's punctuated garment

                                    at the hearing, for you
                          to disappear

                                                from running this
        right here, from running

                                            from, from

                asking body-made, this readymade question is a kind of running from

like hoppers paid by fleeing, without paying, from looking from
another world who settled choirs, them harpers, miss bama, unowned
in one another, round, unled,

I pay attention so I won't appear,
bottle-necked, wachovia-tracked,

with a notice on my door
'bout putting notices on doors

3

eastman and jamal had these evil, secret, evil nigger secret meetings in buffalo, but on the run,
but not for me.

      how far away with the sentence can you go, he said. I can go for life, he said,
to the incloser, in her collection, where love is a stranger and her lost mother's
      regulated membership.

      social death is a house party for smart people,
   for holy fools in wilmington and the eastern cape,
     'cause monks refuse at rest at study in silence in the desert snow and then say come again

            come on, get it!

     which is prettier than all the world, and jerome's
     head, which is another rose, and sweet basil of caesarea,
         which reminds me of the way sal said this is *my* pizzeria, against
         his own rule in love and
               say
           again and again and
          then say come again.

3.1

security is sober in his black suit and military brevet. he had a chance to go to germany

          already in panama, but his time out from that fruited, watchful
movement is cordial to the infestation

            of the neighborhood. his creditors

drive by with delicat and speed,

                          past iglesia

          pentacostal shalom, whose image

      is held by pikes

         for the black jews of el salvador,
            in the front yard barbecueing.

it's like a house party for fast,
irremedial social life

is released

then the pedal

4

in studio, at sam cooke's theory of yesterday, till we get out with nothing in reserve, read on sending
till you on your way and I'll rub you till you get that little curve to speak in tongues. this contact
                                                                                        till the single line
        go haywire slid
like that dance his boy kept trying to teach gale sayers in wichita

        but he couldn't do it till that time in philadelphia, when the stone got rolled away from

under mother
bethel and a pan with the grease still warm and a mandolin and brandon labelle and

                                                                        the blue
belles and big maybelle and maybelle

        carter runnin' ever since as smooth off
course on franklin field, in the edge's miracle cut back
        like a school
        of arrangement

from the territory:

braxton switches and railroad ties with arrangement from the territory:
                                    the magic word's machine in ghost computable

    numbers in my head, earpiece made of depth charge, a piece of brick

    is the rocket in my head, the mcnair scholar's tallised song up in my head of
    switches, did she wave in the air of switches, that song of rockets, that pierces every bone:

           our tuned thorn runs through ground rent
and museum
        to come from, as john akomfrah's hands,
his dial toned
        value, his pipe shop songs for not
beginning's open end
        to illustrate our curiosity, our lalia, our
lavalail, theaster,
        our hotmail, our panafrican machine, our
           birds in hand,
        our burning, our birmingham, our
birmingham, our echo:

                                                        where equivalence
            breaks down in song switches, whose obscenity is our drag, our intersection,
                                    our bringing out the grainy motet in us

with an elgin movement

                                    till the citizens rise up
in funmi's remix—nobody can see inside her view—to get down for an instrumental song, a stretch

                                                of 6.2 or 6 or 7 that won't amount as
                        veering
                            come back to life   in a grammar of being suffered,

                                    like the
                                    one who flies apart in
                                    Thematthewprice

            and the beautiful black blonde thing
                of destiny birdsong.

5

maybe lizbeth is a thorn activist. when the world's

        no fair, and has thorns,
      she cuts thorns.

                       or a moog
          or a new jet engine, no eye-focus, no body-focus, but tomorrow

               on a concrete bank

    our essay, life and force,

   her quinceañera in the pines, then
amar, then

   beryl.

they play
it on a minor
lute, the string's
intestine
struggles buzz with small intention, flown in octaves
like octavia, her various release, and wes montgomery's and monk
montgomery's groove-elaborate tension, stark candy of the
stubblefields, orange and yellow on the ground.

perry is hiding in my tummy. I'm lois scott. I sound her lungs, her daddy's
sound, your mama's daddy's lungs'
black lonesome
sound. is she your mom, is that her gun,
yeah, the high commonness of our collection, armed for transition, love to sing, love to shoot.

they don't exist 'cause I'm a kid. I want

two babies,
I'm holding them, they would come visit, to look at a tree

and then to bridge and I would
get them toys and steal their shoes with coal
because my social pleasure rhymes with them.

maybe bessie
is a thorn
activist. when
she put a circle
on the way you wander,
sharper now,
the way you chart and turn to
devastate, she takes turns.

6

stark, impossible
deliberate, to all y'all in west oakland, greetings, in
the name.

none was expected but you know, you should know
he came

as early, sharpeville now, verse one pm,
to savor in

amazement the deliberate tase,

remember,
not just fire.   in every mouth we save alternate drum, now one more time

in cicatritic letter
apostle, deliverer,

got down on time, a band, a village, tell your ma, take you back,
communipaw, the open field of 22

by four by cecil, eight more on the bottom, live
evil, in love with cars, carnal, his other pulse

and flatted growl, præsthetic lunge

and bowl, her sweets

to liquefy, for comedy, a kernel,

bright like a motherfucker.

motherfucker this easy flow beneath our living room. the people in me
stop by to keep on going, deep enough to persevere. it's not that it could only
happen here. our study group is moves for different strings, itinerant piedmont flew
rooted cellar in provence, mississippi on the verge. that undercolonial crop in bright,
mississippi is a storm surge. there go bright olive morris on a brixton pound. saints
preserve our joint communiqué and rêve if you still fugue and rev

motherfucker I love cars. I love to struggle with cars. I love it when rusty
cars won't start for me and when yellow cars won't stop for me. I want to be buried
in one so I can rise in one. I want to be born in one so I can be buried in one. this
tore-up shit means I'm not you. if it ain't got but two tires with tread on 'em can it be
a bicycle? if my eight-track work, come on ride with me to look at them new rims.
you may not have a car at all, miss ella, your groceries, my jitney, and the singers all
intimate in all languages

motherfucker the lock on my front door. when I used to roll with belgrave in pontiac and rouge, stunned multiple when the water wanna go, the elegant squat of an interstate tractor, o, hear the low humn of the ho of the sullen, stolen, rippled ass. here because we brought you here because they brought us here, here with your tiny ears, can't you hear miss ella giving time like dove?

embedded
roach, to all y'all in west sag, fuck y'all, in   the world

                                                comes out your mouth so small
                        the name.   and counted when   you let your songs
            neotoque pall, errandt pusher, unrefined   get old

buzzer, that nigga in the alley's official
                        putation,   potions, when

                                                you drink too many thin

                                    on your own supply.

7

we couldn't afford it but we got some anyway.
the finance company is a superdome. this is
important: did anybody *come* in there?

he snuck in my house like it was mine
and tried to take it away while I was steady
giving it away out of no way and spread out
everywhere. but he couldn't lift what he was in
'cause he wasn't really in it. just a box held
open air all by himself. when all the other cubes
share he's all alone, like juan williams.

so why not take what they been giving all along
and throw it all away on stage, go home
mad, and calculate for shortbread and insurance?

8

to julian's duet, is my barrette and cabaret, is larryette's boulez and tj's lafayetted
renegade pedal and caplet
we engraved for you,

remade his
flute today, enfolding perry in his tummy, reconstructed
with himself to play. today black music comes from rainbow to the deep and spanish out to where it's held by
flightlings, who study changes. you don't have elegies for migrants. you sing a song of sticks for jams, a pit to
form, extravagant as nur, to nur's way

9

I grew up in a bass community in las vegas.
everything was on the bottom and everything was
everything and everybody's. we played silos. our propulsion
was flowers. the cellar was flooded with raised sand. johnny
winter in america. everybody and everything was hard again.

daddy was a street corner. mama was a market woman. miss lady tore up everybody
about her grass. we ground each other sometimes and chased each other and got
down with everything. a lot of our skin was on the ground and we talked about each
other. leslie would cap against his name and around the corner and up at the store
st. francis and upper room standing around, christ in olive and kamenev's open seed.

louie vitale and sister mary. willie stargell and stephanie brown. lisé and boderick,
margaret, ousmane and jameela. deseretta mcallister. julia cotton and brian jackson
tennessee and scottie heron. greg robinson was lou rawls live. brother mike was the
queen of chanting and typing. penley park was chuckie pleasant. chuckie pleasant

was giant eagle. giant eagle don't believe in them airplanes. some of us believed and left our homes
and came looking. everybody on the ground and everything
was left. st. james still there and disappeared.

9.1

in a window in the sound escape but what if it's a wardrobe, a blue strap set of looks in military qipao
for my weave and fade or shag, or even lightning of the black
skein that holds it all together, hip tight, a discipline of hips, in bottom's thick partition.

9.2

look how song and dance don't go together down the avenue. soon as we call this line derailment we'll study
service, no eye-focus, no body-focus, then get down together. like an ancient decision
with ragin playing through, we accent the second syllable because we are disciples, o harpsic flugel'd refuge,

9.3

with some audiovisual shape to us, and aerated, in the event of color, long set circle, we revel in what breaks us up.

      with nothing it's impossible and easier, the same but really close to one another but unbridgeably far

    from one another, the way we flee a broken park when the island

     is a shipwreck and a language lab and half of school falls away. for what we live for

       little boy removed, upstairs, a choir down below. how to read this is double now. *now,*

how do we read this? this is what it's for. to claim catastrophe

  to rubble for catastrophe.   to turn the world

this
ain't   what
            is, look,
this   is
    what

            9.31

    ain't assert
break, insert, say
everything?

9.4

the pardoner is more textual than I am
  empirical. my bag is from st. louis, on tour,
        got down on folded doors. the thing, the one,
  surround me in the clear, on funky side,
           to let me make me mean something this year,

      I mean to make something else all the time.
  the harder you look inside
       the easier it is to forget about gary. black youth has
always been a project of sonic youth in the
everyday distortion. we clear? sharper? my
  plan is based on human nature, from tutu
         to biko, with a continental burst in my
  gig bag, which is keene-toed, sharp as a tack

on jump, bent, that you reveal in brokenness,
         that it was something there to pass, on tour,
    and come to pass it on there every night.

10

we live beneath ourselves as julianic monsters fighting monsters with smiling.
social life is science fiction and it keeps on being new like seeing sails.
you throw shade on doorways but we love doorways.
we have to live this way. we love to live this way.
science fiction is bottom's retrovroom and thickening.
loaded inside and out with violence and sugar and contemplative food and hunger for overabundant black
cake,

extra in the pre-history of the music, and in the emily of wealth and taste,
domingo is the ancient capital of spice. women spike and peak meringue,
my stops and frets and struts and fretwell's haitian fight song,
euphonicaption probably won't survive the shot.
the logic board perimeter, perry, perry, my perrymeter, machine of my inside, makiko in the gap,
we wanna know what makes the students move, from kyoto to amherst to fayetteville to gdansk.
maybe cake is the only way for this telegraphic message, from you to groove and tongue and nail, the collective
4tet.

11
I'm in a bad mood about
everybody's bad mood, their
political depression, whatever.

and they're so god damn
squeamish about it — they
can't even come close to

saying how fucked up it is,
with their anempathic
numbers, but they can say
that. they so attached

to it but they can say that.
o, say what they cannot can!
to say there's no exit from
compromised ordinariness

is an ordinary compromise,
as if there's more danger in the
idea of flight than in staying

home, as if laying back where
you stay precludes flying, as if
the symposium were theirs alone,

my improvisitor, through black
white sun, that music gave me
to mark me, my own awning,

mobile, at miss starks's house,

drummer some a patch
of dirt behind it, yard

assembly dance the feel
trio of emelle, singing

that beautiful relation in missippi between specific and pacific, (o amazing hit, breathing es, this sustenance wadada held to give, not
    lost, becomes a diphthong in work, gliding are, to common granaries of the other sun, but I didn't know, it lookeded
  beautiful to me, ahead, like mykah and lorenzo at the future, in leland, inside out of the other sun 12. we are the cult of flor in error,

banquet, gallery. we depend on plants not to work to rule, to volunteer to repudiate the genevan, unsung to smithereens, with a personal
      haint and ivy. this overcome from under keep having come just yesterday, just like forever. the plasticity of plants and the sisters
  who tend them is something to see, through black white sun, when they breathe in circles, to work this thing, because it is our pleasure.

I ran from it and was *still* in it.

I come from around to just above angola excape. song
is homeless for running away inside. make us clear the
stumps and squats and raise shit up on a brutal echoed
bottom. we don't feel comfortable till we step and till
in them public private clubs. then the fish scent hit the

air that we turn over. then we take the latest thing up
to bring back new things. then move secret in the city
that repeat it every time we come and send. then curve
the gated embouchure and a key made out of combs to

amuse you with flavor. then solfège at the poor theater.

then reels but for real we don't play but curl up in boxes.

I found the cover art for the aftermath. this head is a

whole other studio. dispose is unreal but this phrase is

too distant. we was all set to run. fall was reset to run.
but hey mr. man how you? my sad parole, or turn here
or turn here, before the parole board, on a whole other
clef, my bent grammar, they did a sonogram of my cell
for the flavor-logged horscape and curved phrase inside
and again I was denied, called out my name, though el
is the name of my game. in the name of the black cube,
when I get out I got to go to 13 bars. it's more than 13
bars in this one bar. my new sky song for is for you, suh.

I used to drive soul wynne to the tavern every got damn
night so I know he just wanted to kill as many devils as
possible. annular spring and broken circle was a rubber
band—not instead of killing devils but actually sprung,

dropping motherfuckers off in shadow, on the outskirts
of ceased, at the edge of that cool move, then wash our
hands at our wash stand. at the end, you know, I had to
buy him a pair of shoes. they buried him in liberty city

but nobody came. something about the music the music
curls up in boxes yeah but stretched out quietly with his
head off to the side like it would when he was singing

I make no mistake. make you wanna turn around and take her ass to the airport. I need to run by the beauty shop so pull over here so I can get me some cigarettes. let me get up from here—you almost let me forget to get my check. ride up to the 7-11 and get me some now or laters. it better be too clean in here when I get back. you better not come back up in here without my paper. As soon as she get back here I think I'll pack my bags and head that way. I'll eat whatever ya'll got if it's some pig feet. ooooh, I wish a motherfucker would try to put his foot on me. mad at you 'cause your feets too good.

I pray to the elegant string. of off-handed evenness,
the window is a soma you talk through. what music
you'll become and the beautiful cars you'll drive! the
frontier that invades you for singing. the driven curl
of an inside opening. all the elegant lines turn to and
from themselves. for you become the turn with your
own fly ornaments. the curve in between the edge of
town and silence bent down to the muted floor. just
like every other lover of the bottom, the elegant lover
of the bottom, miss thing of the sound border, in the
end fly past the object, gathering, and cant my prayer.

I can't keep my hands from myself or my eyes on you.
last night I wrote a book called *Swiss Kross: Evacuation
Bridge*. see the broke villagers celebrate while bop and
fig get down, secretly. upstairs, housekeeping get on
down. get it down on paper napkins and matchbooks

and keno tickets. got to get down on it on the islands

to give it up at the landmark. get some at the stardust

in the new form of sonny criss. get to go off like trains,
dance in the slant economical sanctuary with the moon

on it. come on get it with the fluted ride in the shining
lounge. akLaff is still some kind of still self-stimulation.

I call the other one *beauty in sets* to mark how you blow
rings through l and l, my little all, and still, for the feel
and then roll up on the other one all full. party people
in the place to be, my fly francophonofilic phonograph
tore it up with the melody nelson and a mute cut from

a carafe. come turn a circle on your little jimmy. come

twirl the corner of the table. come edge and cymbal on
my grain. let me feel your tip with the come edge circle
run. come feel my shoulder just to see if you still feel me
all and all. I think it's separated. I think you undergiven.

you gon' walk away without telling me what to call you?

I burn communities in shadow, underground, up on the
plateau, then slide with the horny horns. vision's festival
is folded in overtones and outskirts. j tizol, harry carnival
and feel lined out around an open forte, an underprivilege
of the real presence, curled up around an outlaw corner.
curling around corners puts me in mind of jean toomer.
I think I'll change my name to gene tumor. I want to be
a stream tuner, unfurled in tongues that won't belong in
anybody's mouth, mass swerving from the law of tongues,
let me slip my slap-tongued speech in your ear, the burnt
starry star of all love in your ear. o, for a muse of fire music.

I want to work each other remotely, open the other
thing on the way home all the time, brush when you

drive the moon and other things below the seat stir,

another form of life outside your door this evening,

after the phone call to your mama's house, the cold
water dripping from your hair, the floor in between
everybody's bed on the road and the wall, on top of
that desk nobody writes on, past the hall where the
danish curl, on the edge of the frozen lot with your
hair dripping, out on the open highway, electric on
your slick buttons, a soft little orange breath on you.

I threw my shade down like a windowpane. on the
borders and cloth rises, off in the music's renegade

thicknesses, soft thighs, black elbows. and crossed

up your science except for the part that can't find

enough particles. this is the edge of an organic line

that loves each other in the cistern. it's another city
up in the waves and that cleanhead man is singing it
right now! everybody grounding, everybody making
strings out of curls with open tuning in response. John
hears it like a natural communist shadow, madly in

love with all that wealth and flow on jackson street.

I wish for other singing. here go three yellow balls,
a whirl and bounce, and a little pretending. up and
down ain't reached for singing yet or it seem like it.

not even no and yes every once in a while with mis

opuestos and mis colores. but when there's another
singing that I wish for that he sings or that I wish I
wish for past the cold pragmatics. pray for that little
monkish tilt you run to edge from and bolt the way
he kisses money. sing the box to curl. contredance
make they camera shake off that mulch and switch
to another quadrant. this is a story about his music.

I saw tshibumba blue all blue in the western sky. that
anagreen make culver city radiate past all the native

grasses. lumumba and ince are reading on an island,

off washington, on governing, for grandeur. how the
grasses burn in culver city when the flame is blue. it's
the piano in a bakery they can't sit in. they can sit in
but they can't stay there. they can stay there but they
can't live there. can you take ince to manchester to
the airport? they can fly there but they can't work it.
they can work there but they can't buy shit. form a
revolutionary distance in the mode of blue in green.

I run with code that's a matter of tone. the way avery
brooks keep happening to platt as a haunted orator in
tall gestures. that low tone, so come with it, you got it.
another degree of freedom, not enough to get us from
the screen to the woods, but that code. my brane is fly
'cause it holds me. thin won't curl, then shell but won't
curve in panic, for the mystical kernel. my city beside
the river of deep-ass rivers for a hundred miles and the
underground too heavy to count, like spartacus. this is
my teacher's blue black portrait, turned away when the
jam is paused, in depth and pitch to ornament my cell.

I was talking to sandra about her mama. she said her

mind told her to go to nordstrom's and try on some

clothes. she said I need to do these things. she said
she always loved clothes anyway. she said I don't know

why I still got sense with my kids and my mama and
my auntie. my kids think I'm crazy. everybody think

I'm crazy. I don't know how I still got sense. my mind

told me I ain't got no sense. boy, I'm so crazy I'm sleepy,
baby girl. baby, I'm your fool, boy. girl, my mind told my
daughter you need to come take your children and go
home. let me get this sleeping water. welcome, margarita!

I need to get closer to jesus and I wonder if he can

spread out for me. his broken sisters loved me more
than anything. my arms were open wide. now here I

am between reaching and telling you about it again

but not even there or even inside that. invent what I

have where jesus comes to me for lorenzo to speak

to me. then mama and mimi and papa and daddy
will come for me. like rick rubin's commune with
johnny cash every night on the telephone. get away
from here by kissing my otherworldly little boy. now
here he is between fleur between flight and words.

I never learned to swim. my downstroke is a braided
flood plain. spooked by free range white in space,
hiding in leopard print on their head like food for
regular mercenaries, this is my text for the black
shadows keep moving out of shade. they crack on all
the other ones moving in theory like a buoy. when a
hand turn to a crooked stick like a cloud then a lot

of folks troubled by water. we haven't lived here for

a long time and this loop, this boom, this line is my
anti-system love call. the m stands for dancing, and

trailing, her moving, the stylistics of a runaway drell.

I thought about you as the new science. the diluted

gravity of edward witten ran but still and held but fly
like in the curly curve of never starting or stay with
her repeating to go where cities burn each other
quietly. by the bend in the river but hope for the
best. don't take the beginning for baby dodds' urge
circular pause. he'll come to see you too sometimes
she said. and I promise they'll come to see you too
before you even know them. you won't test the new

theory of the parallel till they hold your hand, maybe

tonight. I hope they're in there with you right now.

I turn forty-four like leroy kelley but dug in. the fat
middle is like twenty-two in the afterlease. up in the
joint of protesting joints and unreliable joints and too
old to smoke but every once in a while I be smokin'

but small and unsustained like marvis frazier. you want

your kids to be better than you but still love you when
the prophets are mean to you. slide away in the crowd

having felled no trees as dennis edwards in the burning

earliness. you no other flower in the world. you like a

rose but lost to the world. black art is late work. before
every other thing but off to the side in the thing of it is.

I got something that makes me wanna shout. it goes
off in another chemistry, preserves off the set in a
black vein of fresh cream. flavor refreshes life by
going off. the unsaved ones save you, buried over the
edge of aroma, my flower. atmosphere seem so clean
now, we can really get together. I got something
that tells me what it's all about. my world is such a
beautiful place. every sound is curled up in my arms
then the band drives her to the rainbow edge. look,
my soul looks back. soul, tell me how to save that
burning getting over. I got soul and I'm super bad.

I throw the eloquent vulgarity of florence of flesh
from shoal to curl. here go the transcript for some
changes. here go some curling iron. here go my baby
picture. here go bright wilbur morris walking on and
on in nowhere. that new air lit out for the territory
band. I found live at pope's tavern at the downtown
music gallery. that's on black saint. the white guelph
album on soul note. everything else on atlantic, I mean
under it, you know, on the gallery floor. the holler we
mean to put air in is exile. our shit is a pallet on the
gallery floor or fire or flor or banquet that union hall

I often amount to no more than a stylistics. airrion

love and uncountable son and I want to amount to
nothing more than that. my gift is more than you
can carry. all other things are just my style. my thing
is everything is everything and there's nothing more

than my bouquet, my uncountable thing outside. my

voices inside blow up inside a blackening gift from a
broken hand. we were cagey in our bib caps and our
overcoats carried the hidden weight of our broken
circle. lost city people make the world go round.
remember that time at the marriott wardman park.

I carry the particles from market to market. I can't
lose with the stuff I use. my essence presses lightly

down on presencing. the incomplete victory sound

like enough to me but still and all it's real heavy to

sing with broken records. to get shit hooked up to a
free response. to mythically lift your hand differently
as rhythmically as everything. to take a little break in

lygia, arkansas and still folded in jerome, arkansas and
the broke distillery at cummins. to carry over the lost
mass inside but open. I always be the thing presenting
broken jam particles. I come from the city of markers.

I like to put a surprise in your lunchbox just for you.
I know you'll know the resonator, and a good, strong
piece of peppermint, and how that go all the way back
to lake mead and engelstad. you can put moves inside

little bits of colored paper and put it in a chest for all

their friends to open up and not remember. say a little

prayer for you is a love song from mother to son and

that's cool and you know that. if I hold my hand to my

cheek when I breathe her name that's like a piece of
hard candy in your lunchbox and your cell block. I like
to be able to give you these things from time to time.

I circulate babylon and translate for the new times.
secret runway ads brush and cruise each other and
the project runaway. in the brocade and panache of
intuitions, and their bracketed patterns we wait to
boom, their hands poise chiffon and counteract red
fleece. their perro is a stone, a pedro flying down a
red top with a blue scarf flying. this is all limited by
mama's black beads, one give him comeuppance on
the bottom lip. between that one and that one that
rub that thread, a uniform of tongued blemishes and
star frets on slideways, my old guitar just love to sing

I can't love nobody but the poor. misunderstanding
pan tuning is our luxury. we need a little ointment
on the edge. our mannered labor wear the work out

that the people always gather when they play mas.

even if nobody wants to be out here but you it's ok.

when you sing what you don't know how to say the

saying turns. we buried all of 'em on less than that.
we turned away from the grave and fell out. and now
you 'bout the only one that know who lucille is. that

know where lucille is. that have no place to go. that
sometimes we just turn and brush our hands because.

I like to enjoy myself. I enjoyed you, fred. 'cause we tell
stories. 'cause we live in common. every night, live in
stockholm, the secret acceleration of a thousand years
on the road till the particles collide and cry on the
bridge between cern and fermilab, as sacred means.

the theory of enjoyment is in repose, rubbing the history
of broken veins and towels wore down to velvet. the theory
of enjoyment puts itself in danger to remain still, as a part
of breath, while the sails glide. when you can't do no
better, the feeling of the theory of enjoyment is solid.

the experiment of the ones who live to eat enormously.

I am foment. I speak blinglish. at work they call me
but I don't come. I come when she call me by my
rightful name. I come to myself from far away just
laid back in the open. I ran from it and was *still* in it.

it's a blue division on my goodbye window. I'm full
of outer space. I'm free as dred all night. I get clung

with a voice that gets held back by surge protection.

I'm daddy I come when he crazy he call me I'm crazy.
I come when he call me once upon a time in arkansas.
when the water come I come to the unprotected surge
and division in my old-new sound booth. I am fmoten.